BULLIES BE GONE! PROJECT™

Comprehensive Eight-Week Course

STUDENT WORKBOOK

FOR CHILDREN & TEENS
AGES 9–17

AL JOHNSON

Published by
Hybrid Global Publishing
301 E 57th Street, 4th fl
New York, NY 10022

Copyright © 2017 by Al Johnson

All rights reserved. No part of this book may be reproduced or transmitted in any form or by in any means, electronic or mechanical, including photocopying, recording, or by any information storage and retrieval system, without the written permission of the Publisher, except where permitted by law.

Manufactured in the United States of America, or in the United Kingdom when distributed elsewhere.

Johnson, Al
    Bullies Be Gone! Project: Student Workbook

Cover design by: Joe Potter
Interior design: Claudia Volkman
Illustrations by Shanna Lim

www.bulliesbegoneproject.com

BULLIES BE GONE! PROJECT™

LESSON #1
FOR BULLIES BE GONE PROJECT (A.KA. BBGP) INSTRUCTORS, PARENTS, TEACHERS, CHILDREN, AND TEENS

Instruction to Children: You must practice all BBGP skills as directed to clearly understand and retain the concepts and objectives of each lesson. This will maximize your skills.

Contact Al Johnson at **al@antibullyingexpert.com** or your certified BBGP instructor for questions you may have regarding the subject matter. Your parents or teachers must be notified first, giving you permission to email.

History of the Program

This program was created by Al Johnson in 1985 in the Parks & Recreation Department of Manhattan Beach, CA. Originally, it was called The Young, Alert, and Aware Program, (YAA) a Six (6) week comprehensive training, for ages 5-15.

In 2008, Al Johnson renamed the YAA program to The Bullies Be Gone! Project (BBGP) an Eight (8) week comprehensive training, for ages 9-17. Al Johnson has single-handedly taught thousands of children, teens, and adults in California anti-bullying, safety, awareness, self-confidence, and racial harmony vital life skills since its inception.

Objective of the Bullies Be Gone! Project:

Self-Empowerment Training for Children and Teens that Prevents and Protects Against Bullying

Physical Fitness Warm Up Exercises

In the Eight-Week Comprehensive Bullies Be Gone! Project training, specific fitness exercises will be taught to you. As a child or teen, you should consistently practice the fitness techniques taught in class. **(At least twice weekly)**

Explanation by Instructor/Parent and Reasons Why Physical Fitness Is Important:

- A physically fit child's self-esteem may be positively impacted.
- **Escaping from and/or controlling** a bully may be easier if you are physically fit.
- Successfully running from a threatening situation with a bully may be the results of being physically fit. (**"Emergency Running Skills"**—which will be taught in this training)
- Having the appearance of being physically fit may be enough to prevent a bully from ever approaching you in a threatening manner.
- Having the appearance of being physically fit helps you display **Powerful Body Language**, which will be taught in this training.

Awareness Training:

Your Teacher/Parent will ask you what **Awareness** means to you and what does it mean to be Aware?

Do you know what it means to be Keenly Street and Internet Aware? **(Your Teacher/Parent will discuss with you)**

Keen Street, School, and Internet Awareness will be taught to you in this training, as well as Role Playing, and numerous ways **Awareness** applies to **Bullying**.

1. **Children and Teens:** In the Bullies Be Gone! Project Training, you will be told several true **Stories** relating to Awareness, Bullying, and your Safety.

2. Our first story references **Awareness, Thinking on Your Feet (Explained by Instructor) and being Street Smart.** These are important elements in making sure you learn skills and techniques to **Effectively Eliminate or Prevent** being bullied.

Story #1 is about Al Johnson at age 15:

How he immediately put into action **thinking on his feet with awareness skills, avoiding** a threatening bullying situation, while walking out his front door on the way to school. He was confronted by 3 bullies. (Your teacher/parent will tell you the story) Make sure you listen carefully and take MENTAL NOTES!

The following Awareness Poem and Illustration is the first Instructional piece you will learn to help you begin to Eliminate and Prevent Bullying:

WORDS, PHRASES, and STANZAS in **Bold Print** in the body of the poem should be discussed after the poem is read. These are important to the **Theme and Main** idea of the poem. Your Parent/Teacher will guide you through the process.

Your workbook contains all the poems for each week's lesson. You should memorize **key words, phrases, stanzas, theme(s) of poems**, and the **entire poem for best results.**

You will learn and develop POWERFUL WORDS of responses to a bully's negative WORDS and build self-confidence and self-esteem, whether **face to face with a bully or online.**

You must continue to study the poems and illustrations which may have hidden messages for your **recall, retention, and review**.

Oral and written responses of poems and questions will be asked of you during the training.

The reading and training aspects of poems proceed as follows:

Your Parent/Teacher will guide you through the process:

First: You will be directed to take a close look at each **Illustration**. What is the illustration saying to you? Are there any hidden message/s in the illustration?

Incentive for you learning and reciting the poem in front of the class: (If applicable – your parent/teacher may or may not use this incentive)

A trophy will be given for the BEST performance determined by the class via silent ballot vote. Trophies will be presented at the end of the 8-week training. Everyone will have an opportunity to win over the 8-week course. Students can perform a maximum of 2 poems in a week's lesson. (One poem at a time recommended) This process is designed to enhance the overall objective of the Bullies Be Gone! Project Training.

Instructors/Parents will explain how this works if you are training with a parent, but not at school.

AWARENESS

What is this illustration's theme and what could be the hidden message/s in the illustration?

AWARENESS

A kid's best chance of not being bullied is to be **keenly aware** of bullies long before it's too late.

Kids must know **subtle signs** a bully might reveal and what those signs could indicate.

Too often today, a kid's attention is **focused** on iPads, cell phones, and any other electronic device.

Kids are not nearly as focused on their **environment**, people in it, or **potential trouble** that could be **lurking** almost in **plain** sight.

Bullies count on kids not being aware. This makes it easy for a kid to be caught off guard.

Being caught off guard, surprised, and confused make chances of avoiding and defeating the bully very hard.

The only good thing about bullies is that they're **easily recognized**, if a kid knows what to look for. Bullies and potential ones **tend** to have **similar traits.**

They call kids names, push and shove, and want things their way. They **seldom** smile and, when **patience** is needed, the bully has none. Bullies are **ill-equipped** to **patiently wait.**

There are other **unpleasant** signs a bully has; those are just an important few.

Kids, please learn to recognize them, you'll be more aware and have a much better chance of avoiding the bully if you do.

Stay alert, stay aware, and stay away from the bully. It's what you must **effectively learn how to do.**

By sharpening your awareness skills, the outcome will be bad for the bully, and a very good one for you.

Al Johnson

AWARENESS VOCABULARY LESSON: Discussion of meanings of the following **WORDS** and how they are used in the stanzas of the poem will now take place:

Keenly aware, subtle signs, indicate, focused, potential, lurking, tend, similar traits, seldom, patience, ill-equipped, unpleasant, effectively, outcome

Awareness is the first of many **VITAL LIFE SKILLS** concepts you will learn in the BBGP training program.

Instructor/Parent will now teach you important **WORDS, PHRASES & STANZAS** from the body of the poem reinforcing the **Theme & Main Idea**, all to Effectively enhance your self-confidence and self-esteem. (These are highlighted in **Bold Print**.)

Discuss with Instructor, parents, and teachers:

The meaning of **bold print words, phrases, stanzas** to effectively offset the impact of **negative words and inappropriate actions** by bullies and to build a **Self-Empowerment Mindset**.

Children and Teens must know and retain the following objective of their training:

Bullies Be Gone! Project Training Objective:

Self-Empowerment Training for Children and Teens that Prevents and Protects Against Bullying

Instructor/Parent will now teach the following:

Instructor/Parent will read the following as students read silently, from their workbook:

The following powerful lesson is designed to teach you exactly what to do immediately if anyone attempts to bully you or you fear being bullied. This technique, along with many others to follow, if learned well, practiced, and retained, will give you a much better chance of permanently preventing or eliminating a bully problem **Effectively and Independently.**

Instructor/Parent will Reinforce the following with you:

To permanently eliminate a bullying problem, you as a child or teen must know how to effectively, (On your own) solve a bullying problem or potential one via **Self-Empowerment.**

HITTING THE LIGHT SWITCH

What is this illustration's theme and what could be the hidden message/s in the illustration?
Hint: The theme is not so obvious. You may have to read the poem first and come back to this illustration for a better understanding.

Instructor/Parent will now read the POEM

After the reading, the instructor will have you go over to the light switch in the classroom or parent at home and instruct as outlined in the poem.

If there is a large group of students, the instructor will go over to the light switch, while instructing students as outlined in the POEM.

Unless at school, under teacher's guidance, this drill is ONLY practiced in the home, with parent's assistance and permission.

HITTTING "THE LIGHT SWITCH"

In this poem, you will learn how **hitting "the light switch"** could help you in a big way get rid of a bully.

Kids, **"the light switch" is in your mind**, a place where a bully cannot touch or see.

You should **only practice** this **drill** at home or with your parent or teacher, which is the proper thing to do.

Their involvement is important, so they can learn with you.

Go over to the light switch in your house; place your **index finger** on it so you can **control** it by **flicking** it back and forth or up and down.

Now, look directly at the lights you are about to make go on and off, those lights in the ceiling or at eye level. While hitting "the light switch," **concentrate, don't look all around.**

Keep your eyes **glued** to the lights as you begin to flick them on and off. Do this very quickly about five or six times.

My question to you is: "How long did it take for the lights to go on and off?" Remember, hitting "the light switch" is all about your mind.

Did the lights go on and off in a matter of seconds, is that what you would say?

You would be correct if you said no more than a second or two. You would be correct in every way.

As a kid, you might be asking what does this have to do with a bully. How does this help me?

Well, I will soon explain **further**, then you will clearly see.

If a bully ever comes around wanting to **hassle** you, **immediately hit "the light switch" in your mind.**

You must do it, if **necessary**, in any bullying situation. You must do it every single time!

Just as quickly as you saw the lights go on and off, you must do the following three things with **ease**:

Relax, React, Respond as fast as the lights went on and off. The complete necessity of this drill you will soon see.

You will be taught the **Three R's** and how to apply them in the next poem's lesson, so you can perform under a **bully's pressure**, and **perform without a glitch**.

From this poem, children and teens MUST learn if a bully **hassles** them, they must immediately know how to **effectively in their mind**, hit "the light switch."

Al Johnson

HITTING "THE LIGHT SWITCH" VOCABULARY LESSON: Discuss the meanings of the following words and how they are used in the poem: Control, flicking, concentrate, glued, further, hassle, immediately, ease, glitch, if necessary

The Theme of the Poem is Hitting "The Light Switch," a metaphor for you to understand the importance of your **MIND** and to effectively and immediately use it when confronted by a bully.

Instructor/Parent will now go over each of the important **WORDS** and **PHRASES** In **bold print** from the body of the poem to reinforce the theme and enhance your self-confidence and self-esteem.

Objective of the Bullies Be Gone! Project:

Self-Empowerment Training for Children and Teens That Prevents and Protects Against Bullying

LESSON #1 SUMMARY:

Meditation for Review, Recall & Retention will now be taught to you.

Method of teaching: Instructor/Parent will guide you through the following process—when you learn it, you can do this on your own as you practice your BBGP skills:

Students will sit in a Yoga (Indian Style, Legs Crossed) position, with their backs perfectly straight, hands resting on their knees, palms up. **You should totally relax.** (More will be taught about how to relax in the next BBGP Lesson.) **Your Instructor/Parent will guide you through this exercise. Listen carefully!**

When you have done the repeating process **five (5) times** with a true understanding of what **Awareness** is and how it applies to bullying, you will be instructed to **open your eyes and quickly stand**, hands behind your backs. **(Similar position like the police would have someone do if they were going to be handcuffed)**

Your Instructor/Parent will demonstrate the process first.

Individual growth and understanding is key to your learning. You are not in competition with anyone but **YOURSELF**!

Standing a certain way **(Hands behind your back, as well as sitting in a Yoga style position)** instills Concentration, Discipline, and Uniformity—important elements in defeating a bully.

Immediately after standing from the **Awareness Meditation** drill, repeat the process with **Hitting "The Light Switch."** As more lessons are taught, you'll be required to Meditate with additional techniques for **Review, Recall & Retention. (Your instructor will guide you through the process)**

It is important from Lesson #1, you: Clearly understand what AWARENESS is and how to immediately **HIT "THE LIGHT SWITCH" in your MIND** if confronted by a bully or anyone else in an uncomfortable encounter.

Reinforcement for Students: You MUST retain the meanings of the **words** and **phrases** for future clarity and understanding and, more importantly, how the **WORDS & PHRASES** are being used in the poem itself.

This overall training is designed to empower you to effectively **Eliminate** and **Prevent** a **Bullying Problem**. You should learn and recite the poems frequently, so **specific words, phrases, and stanzas are ingrained in your mind, much like hearing a new Rap song, listening to it repeatedly, and soon you know all the words.**

Great Emphasis is placed on the following:

YOU ARE NOT TO PLAY with or NOT TAKE SERIOUSLY any of the techniques you learn in BBGP or to SHOW or DEMONSTRATE any of your skills to anyone other than those mentioned below:

You should have **FUN** while learning; however, the training **IS NOT** to be shared with anyone other than instructors, parents, teachers, and other students who are taking the training. (There is one exception in a future lesson and you will be informed)

EMPHASIZING REASONS WHY: When what you learn in this training is PLAYED WITH **(Not taken seriously)** and SHOWN to friends, the techniques WILL NOT WORK in an actual bullying situation.

Reason: You'll have **Exposed** the **ELEMENT OF SURPRISE** in eliminating or preventing being bullied. (If you need further clarity, ask your instructor/parent, or email me directly) The ELEMENT of SURPRISE & DOING THE UNEXPECTED are VITAL COMPONENTS in DEFEATING the Bully!

THE TRAINING IS SERIOUS, yet Enjoyable. IT'S EXTREMELY IMPORTANT YOU UNDERSTAND WHAT YOU LEARN IN THIS COURSE IS YOUR SECRET TO KEEP, and to be used EFFECTIVELY as instructed if you're ever find yourself in an UNCOMFORTABLE situation with a bully.

Next Lesson's Training:

- Review Lesson #1 (By Instructor)
- The 3R's & How to effectively apply them in a bullying situation
- Mental Toughness & How it applies to bullying and its importance

END OF LESSON #1

Lesson #2
For BBGP Instructors, Parents, Teachers, Children & Teens (This will be the continuation of Lesson #1)

1. **Review Lesson 1** — Awareness & Hitting "The Light Switch"

2. **Physical Fitness** Warm Up Exercises (approx. 10–15 minutes)

3. **Share with your Instructor/Parents any occurrences** during the week since the last class requiring use of your BBGP skills. Did you witness or were involved in any Bullying situations or potential ones where Awareness & Hitting "The Light Switch" came into play? (Discuss)

   If there were incidents, your teacher will offer any suggestions to make the situation better if a repeated or similar incident occurs. (As needed)

   The 3R's and how to apply them will now be introduced by you instructor.

   Students read along with the instructor:

   The following powerful lesson is designed to teach you exactly what to do immediately if anyone attempts to bully you or you fear being bullied.

   In Lesson #1, you were taught about Awareness & Hitting "The Light Switch" in your Mind and introduced to the **3R's (Relax, React, Respond)**. Now you will be taught exactly how to use the 3R's against a bully.

   This skill, if learned well, practiced, and retained, will give you a much better chance of **Eliminating** or **Preventing** a bullying problem permanently!

Here are the **3R's** again, and you **MUST NOT** ever forget them. They are Life Long skills! You will be asked later in the training what the **3R's** are and how to apply them as well as all the skills and techniques you will be learning.

Students under the direction of your instructor will now repeat the **3R's** one at a time, with enthusiasm and conviction:

Relax, React, Respond

You will now learn the application of the 3R's in an encounter with a Bully or anyone making you feel uncomfortable.

RELAX, REACT, RESPOND

What is this illustration's theme and what could be the hidden message/s in the illustration?

Just as in Lesson #1: Parent/teacher will now read the poem as the 3R's are being taught to you. The underlined is not part of the poem, but instructions on what to do to enhance the necessary training of the 3R's after certain stanzas. Your instructor will guide you through the process.

RELAX, REACT, RESPOND

Okay, class, in the poem before this one you learned about hitting "the light switch" in your mind to help you defeat the bully, if you must.

I introduced the Three R's, now you're going to learn what they mean and how to put them to good use.

Relax is the first thing you must do if the bully ever gets in your face. "So, how do I relax," you might say?

Take a quick, quiet, deep breath, inhale and suck the air in through your nose, exhale, quietly blow the air out through your mouth quickly. Do it two or three times.

<u>**(Demonstration by Instructor—you will perform relaxation, as you have learned, while sitting & standing)**</u>

Imagine you are pinching a balloon that you just blew air into between your thumb and index finger to keep the air inside.

As soon as you take your finger and thumb away, the air rushes out, the balloon goes **limp** and becomes very relaxed.

By relaxing quickly in a bad situation, especially with a bully, your muscles don't become **tense** and your mind remains clear, now you can better **react**.

<u>**Instructor will demonstrate what tense muscles look like.**</u>

React is to immediately decide how you are going to allow yourself to feel about this unwanted bully situation. Proper relaxation should help you take control.

You will either feel scared or excited, very aware or unaware of your surroundings, confident or not confident, ready or not ready to immediately take control.

(Instructor will emphasize if you do feel excited and scared, you must do so in a controlled fashion—instructor demonstrates a non-controlling reaction.)

You will react in pretty much one of these ways.

Now you must decide how you are going to **Respond**. Your goal is to cause the bully to have a very bad day.

Here are ways you can **Respond**: walk away from the bully as fast as you can, it may or may not be the best solution, and the bully may follow you.

(Instructor will demonstrate the incorrect and correct ways to walk away from the bully. a) By immediately turning your back to the bully to walk away. b) Cautiously walking away)

Run away from the bully as fast as you can, with your purpose being to find a **responsible** adult to help you.

However, unless you've been taught **"Emergency Running Skills,"** this may or may not be a wise thing for you to do.

(You will be taught "Emergency Running Skills in this course.)

The bully could possibly chase and catch you.

If you are caught, the bully will probably be angry, and could get physical with you. Unless you've been trained with proper self-defense and self-confidence skills, this would be an advantage for the bully. (You will be taught these skills in this course.)

If you have the confidence, you can try to talk your way out of the situation. If you choose this response, you must be **stone-faced and look the bully straight in the eyes.**

(Instructor will Role play this scenario with you – this will be a FUN exercise)

If the bully is demanding you give him/her something of yours, you can choose to do so or not. If the bully has a weapon, give them what they want, you must quickly comply.

If the bully has no weapon and he/she decides to get physical with you,

Your last reaction, because you have no other choice, is to get physical, too.

However, to fend off a bully physically may require certain self-defense skills, especially ones where punches are not thrown, but the bully is put under your physical control.

(You will learn controlling and escaping techniques in this course)
You will need specific training to learn these skills so your reaction can be brave and bold.

Relax, React, Respond must be done by you just as fast as the lights went on and off when you were **Hitting "The Light Switch."**

You'll need and receive from this class special training and practice to effectively Relax, React, and Respond in an uncomfortable bully situation, how to do so, and hopefully, without a glitch.

Al Johnson

Reminder to Student:

The 3R's must be done with a **PURPOSE** and must be **INSTINCTIVE** if you are ever confronted with a bully situation or any incident that makes you feel uncomfortable. **(Your instructor will clarify & explain)**

Awareness, Hitting "The Light Switch," and applying the 3R's – Relax, React, Respond, **all must be done in a matter of seconds!**

THE 3R's VOCABULARY LESSON: Inhale, exhale, limp, tense, control, immediately, stone-faced, comply, brave, bold, relax, react, respond, fend, glitch, effectively

Instructor will discuss **WORDS, PHRASES, and STANZAS IN BOLD PRINT in the poem** and how they apply to the theme of the poem.

What do you believe the following phrase in the poem means?

Relax, React, Respond, hopefully "without a glitch" – (Discuss with instructor for clarity)

INTRODUCTION TO: MENTAL TOUGHNESS LESSON

Read Along with Instructor:

The following important lesson is designed to help you begin understanding **the power of your Mind and how you must develop Toughness of the Mind to defeat bullies.**

The bully uses nasty words to destroy your self-confidence, self-esteem, and weaken your mind. **This occurs face-to-face or online.**

If the bully is successful in bullying you, you could have unhealthy and unpleasant thoughts lasting a very long time.

Specific Words and Actions can empower you and weaken the bully's negative hold on you. I want the bully to clearly see you as no longer a victim or potential one.

You're going to be **Mentally Tough** and display **EMPOWERED Self-Confidence** and Self-Esteem a bully CANNOT Penetrate or Deflate.

YOU MUST TRULY BELIEVE YOU ARE EMPOWERED and continue to become mentally stronger. (**If necessary, your parent/teacher will explain:** CONVICTION of BELIEF)

A True Story follows:

Instructor will reinforce a previous story by Al Johnson:

Do You Remember: The story about a 13-year-old girl walking home in broad daylight, passing through a closed car wash and how she unfortunately failed to practice Awareness, Hitting "The Light Switch," or the 3R's, and was taken advantage of?

Mental Toughness Training:

About 5 times, as your parent/teacher counts, you will practice the **inhale, exhale relaxation drill** as you learned it in Lesson #1. Each time, you should breathe in and out quickly. You will lip sync with your eyes closed, **"I am mentally tough."**

The very last time (#5) you inhale, exhale the same way. However, this time you do not lip sync the phrase. You open your eyes, as if looking the imaginary bully straight in the eyes, stone-faced, and say out loud, **"I am mentally tough."**

"I am mentally tough" will be repeated as many times as necessary. (Instructor's discretion)

Instructor Reinforces Being Mentally Tough:

For the rest of your life, no matter the circumstance, never forget that you are and **MUST be MENTALLY TOUGH!**

NO ONE can take that toughness away from you unless you ALLOW THEM TO DO SO! AND YOU ARE NOT GOING TO ALLOW THAT TO HAPPEN!

Instructor Will Reinforce: This technique and all BBGP skills, if learned well and practiced, will give you a much better chance of **Preventing** and **Eliminating** a bully problem permanently, if you follow the instructions taught to you in this course.

Students read along silently as your instructor reads aloud:

You should now begin putting into practice the following with this lesson and those to follow:

- Study the poems, memorize specific powerful stanzas and the entire poem. By doing so, you will become EMPOWERED and the Bully will become weaker and ineffective in your eyes and, more importantly, in your mind.
- Each poem contains **WORDS & PHRASES** to empower you & send powerful defeating messages to bullies, and messages for bullies to IMMEDIATELY CEASE THEIR INAPPROPRIATE BEHAVIOR.
- You must clearly understand the **Main Idea or Theme** of each poem.
- Discuss the poem with your teacher/parents
- Express your point of view of the poem and ask you teacher/parent to express theirs—everyone learns.

Students, you MUST:
- Study the illustration of each poem carefully before and after you read it. There may be hidden messages in each illustration
- What is the illustration saying to you?
- What does the illustration say to your instructor/parent? (Ask them)
- Compare interpretations and discuss.
- Most of all, enjoy while learning skills and techniques in this program, designed to help you develop effective ways of **Preventing or Eliminating** a bully problem via **Self-Empowerment**.
- As you read the poem, imagine you are talking directly to the bully with the **WORDS, PHRASES & STANZAS** in the poem.

- If you ever need to say them directly to a bully, I want you to develop the confidence to do so, if you don't have it now.
- If your confidence is strong now, I want the **WORDS** you learn in the Bullies Be Gone! Project lessons to make you **mentally stronger and more confident.**
- Looking someone straight in the eye as you are talking to them is NOT easy. However, by doing so, you will show a great deal of **CONFIDENCE by STEADY & FOCUSED EYE CONTACT**

Whenever speaking directly to a bully face-to-face, no matter how difficult it is to do, look the bully straight in the eyes with your stone-faced (but relaxed) expression, just as we practiced.

The following should ALWAYS be done with parent, teacher, or instructor assistance, if you DO NOT have permission to respond independently on line:

When you are responding to NEGATIVE WORDS by a bully directed at you **ONLINE, COPY & PASTE WORDS, PHRASES, STANZAS** from specific poems from your Bullies Be Gone! Project Poetry Book and Training Workbook.

While pasting, imagine being face-to-face with the bully, looking the bully straight in the eyes as you paste your response to the bully's negative **WORDS**.

EYE TO EYE

What is this illustration's theme and what could be the hidden message/s in the illustration?

EYE TO EYE

It's not easy looking someone straight in the eyes, especially if it's a bully.

The bully might think my **dog-stare** is a challenge and want to pick a fight with me.

Adults have told me that to go eye to eye with someone shows a **tremendous** amount of self-confidence.

Self-confidence is what bullies want to destroy in a kid, that's a bully's main **intent**.

I always look down or away when the bully gets in my face, and the bully sees the **discomfort and fear written all over me.**

So I'm bullied more and more, giving all the power to the bully.

Next time I'm going eye to eye with the bully. I wonder, will there be a change in his/her attitude?

It may be hard at first to go eye to eye with the bully, but it's something I have to do.

Here's a great thought; the bully may just **crumble** a bit under my **visual pressure**, becoming weaker and weaker as the seconds go by.

I now think I have the **pride, confidence, and high self-esteem** to handle the bully eye to eye.

Al Johnson

EYE TO EYE VOCABULARY LESSON: Dog stare, tremendous, intent, discomfort and fear, crumble, visual pressure, pride, confidence, high self-esteem

My Mental Toughness

What is this illustration's theme and what could be the hidden message/s in the illustration?

MY MENTAL TOUGHNESS

My mental toughness wasn't anywhere to be found **when you started bullying me.**

I didn't think much of myself; **your bullying made me feel small and weak.**

I spent a lot of time being angry and crying. I didn't laugh like before, not very much at all.

You were winning, and what little pride I had left was sinking fast. I felt like banging my head against the wall.

Then my parents told me that bullies might be physically strong, but mentally they are very weak.

They told me to develop my mental toughness, and by doing so, I could easily defeat the bully.

So, I started thinking and really believing I was strong, in body and mind.

And you know what? The more I thought about being mentally tough, the more confidence I seemed to find.

Mental toughness is a powerful tool that all kids should develop, have, and constantly use.

If a bully happens to come into your space, the bully will see, sense, and feel your mental toughness. The bully will know if he/she tries bullying you, they cannot win, no way! The bully is destined to lose.

Al Johnson

MENTAL TOUGHNESS VOCABULARY LESSON: Pride, sinking, develop, constantly, sense, destined

Your Instructor/parent will discuss the vocabulary WORDS with you.

Students: Explain to your instructor the meanings of the phrase and question:

Physically Strong, but Mentally Weak & What does being Mentally Tough mean?

LESSON 2 SUMMARY:

Meditation for Review, Recall & Retention

Method of Teaching: (The procedure as in Lesson #1)

Students: You should sit in a (Yoga Style) position, with your back perfectly straight, hands resting on knees with palms up, and totally relaxed.

You will close your eyes, as before, silently repeating (In your MIND) Awareness, Hitting "The Light Switch," Relax, React, Respond, & Mental Toughness. **You will be sitting and standing as you complete each concept, as in Lesson #1.**

When you complete the repeating process five (5) times for each Key Concept, with a true understanding of how each concept applies to bullying, you should open your eyes and quickly stand, hands behind your back. (Police handcuff position)

Most important is your complete understanding of the CONCEPTS taught in the first two BBGP Lessons. **The Meditation process will be repeated at the end of each week's lesson. (Instructor's discretion)**

Each week you will have additional concepts to **Mentally Review, Recall, and Retain**.

Students: You **MUST Practice** this Mental Retention Drill at least 2 times a week (More if you like) at home on your own or with your parent.

You are to **retain the meanings of the WORDS & PHRASES** for future clarity and understanding and, more importantly, how the **WORDS** are being used in the poem itself.

Bullies Be Gone! Project training is designed to empower you to **Eliminate** and **Prevent** a bullying problem. I want you to learn and recite the poems frequently, so specific **words and stanzas** are ingrained in your mind.

Critical Point of EMPHASIS for Students:

You are **NOT to PLAY** with any of the techniques you learn in BBGP. The training **IS NOT** to be shared with friends (Unless it's a friend who is enrolled in the BBGP course) or anyone else other than parents, teachers, or BBGP instructors. **Practice at least 2 times** during the week all the techniques you have been taught and re-read the poems numerous times for clarity, knowledge, retention, understanding, and **Self-Empowerment.**

Students: When techniques in the BBGP training are **PLAYED WITH or NOT TAKEN SERIOUSLY,** and **SHOWN** to friends or other kids, the techniques **WILL NOT WORK** in a real-life bully situation. If you do so, you will have given up the **ELEMENT OF SURPRISE** in defeating or preventing bullying.

THE ELEMENT OF SURPRISE & DOING THE UNEXPECTED in a bully situation are your keys to Eliminating and Preventing a bullying problem.

THE TRAINING IS SERIOUS (Yet FUN) and **YOUR SECRET TO KEEP** to be used **EFFECTIVELY** as instructed if you're ever put in an **UNCOMFORTABLE** situation with a bully or anyone else seeking to take advantage of you!

Next Lesson's Training:
- Review Lessons #1 & 2 (By Instructor)
- Body Language (How it applies to Bullying)
- SIC (How it applies to Bullying)
- Street Smart Awareness Training
- Cyberspace, Online Bullying (Ways to eliminate, prevent, and respond)

END OF LESSON #2

Lessons 3 & 4
For BBGP Instructors, Parents, Children & Teens

Physical Fitness Warm Up Exercises (approx. 10–15 minutes)

Reinforce and Review: Awareness, Hitting "The Light Switch," the 3R's & Mental Toughness, and their importance in BBGP training

Students Discuss with your Parents/Teachers: Any occurrences during the week since the last class that required the use of any of the skills you have learned in the first two lessons of BBGP training.

Did you witness or were involved in any Bullying situations or potential ones? If there were incidents, discuss with your parents/teachers how you responded to the situation.

Students: Specific **Words, Phrases, and Stanzas** can mentally empower you and weaken the bully's negative hold on you. I want the bully to clearly see you as no longer being a victim or potential one.

You're going to be **keenly aware and mentally tough** with **STRONG** and **CONSISTENT** self-confidence and self-esteem that a bully cannot penetrate or deflate.

HOWEVER, YOU MUST ALWAYS BELIEVE WITH CONVICTION THAT YOU ARE.

If BBGP training is learned well and retained, you will have a much better chance of **Eliminating or Preventing** a bully problem permanently.

Students, you must continue to do the following with all lessons in BBGP training:
- Study the poem, memorize the poem for your empowerment and the bully's weakness.
- Each poem contains words, phrases, and stanzas to empower you and send powerful messages to bullies to cease their inappropriate behavior.
- Make sure you understand the main idea or theme of each poem.
- Discuss the poem with your instructor/parents expressing your point of view of the poem and ask them to express theirs – everyone learns by doing so.

Students:
- Study the illustration of each poem carefully before and after you read the poem. There may be hidden messages in each illustration that were not initially seen.

- What is the illustration saying to you and what does it say to your parents or teacher?

- See if your parents/teachers see what you see in the illustration and the poem itself.

- Most of all enjoy learning BBGP skills and techniques to help you develop effective ways of **Eliminating or Preventing** a bullying problem permanently. For this to occur, you must learn, practice, and retain **the empowering messages sent with the poetic words & phrases, along with all BBGP skills & techniques.**

Each time as you read a poem, imagine you are talking directly to the bully with the words in the poem. (Some poems are obviously speaking to the Bully) If you ever have to say them face to face with a bully, you MUST develop the confidence to do so with conviction, if you don't have it now.

If your confidence level is strong, I want the words you learn in all Bullies Be Gone! Project lessons to make you even mentally stronger and more confident.

Students, your Instructor will now introduce SIC and how it applies to Bullying, Awareness, the 3R's, Hitting "The Light Switch," and Mental Toughness:

- In an emergency situation causing you to feel uncomfortable, especially with a **Bully** or someone trying to take advantage of you **mentally or physically, three (3) things almost always occur:**

- **They are:** The acronym **SIC** (Pronounced "Sick")

- **Students:** Do you have an idea what the **S** stands for, the **I**, and the **C**? **Your instructor/parent will explain SIC**.

- **If you did not, SIC =** Surprise, Intimidation, Confusion

- Remember this story from Lesson #1: The 13-year-old young lady was walking home across a car wash in broad daylight and was approached by a man seeking to do her harm?

- In her situation, SIC certainly came into play—Instructor/Parent will demonstrate how

Students:

If you are ever in a threatening situation of any kind, especially with a Bully, **you MUST IMMEDIATELY apply 2 of the elements of SIC,** using all skills you have learned relating to Awareness, Hitting The Light Switch, 3R's & Body Language.

Students: Can you guess which two (2) elements of SIC you MUST apply?

They are: S = Surprise, C = Confusion

- **I = Intimidation** should be used ONLY when **physical controlling** or **escaping** techniques are used

- **Students:** You must reverse **SIC** the bully applies by **DOING THE UNEXPECTED—Bullies DO NOT like THE ELEMENT OF SURPRISE & CONFUSION**

Instructor will Introduce Body Language Training:

- You parent/teacher will now check your Body Language and guide you through the process—Listen carefully and follow directions
- You will be asked to stand in your normal standing position
- **Your Body Language will improve from this training**
- **Students: You will be asked to** repeat several times with conviction, **Body Language**
- **Students:** Your Parent/Teacher will explain why your **BODY LANGUAGE** is very important as it applies to Bullying

Students: The following 2 true stories relating to Body Language will be presented to you via video:

1. Al Johnson being at the police station, seeing and hearing a middle-aged man being **interrogated** who had been in and out of jail most of his life for committing crimes against children **(Body Language related)**
2. Al Johnson strolling through the mall while being watched (unknowingly) by a lady in the mall and what she said to him as he came abreast of her **(Body Language related)**

Students: Your body language and how you appear to others could be the difference in a bully or anyone else approaching you with bad intent. Or they could quickly decide not to approach you because of **the powerful signal your body is sending to the Universe: Your Outstanding and Magnificent Body Language.**

Students: Practice having good body language for the rest of your life. **You should even tell your parents how important body language is to them as adults. (Just in case they don't already know)**

Today children, teen, and adults are constantly walking with poor body language because of eyes glued to their I-phones and numerous electronic devices.

Because of this, they are easy prey for anyone wishing to do them harm.

Instructor will demonstrate:

Another story follows to help you mentally remember, develop, and maintain good body language for the rest of your life:

1. **Video Presentation:** About a 12-year-old girl on stage with Al Johnson and how Al immediately improved the girl's body language from poor to self-confident.
2. You will be given instruction on how the **"Name of Your Street Drill will help improve your body language"** (Depending on your age, another example may be used)

    You will be instructed on how to use the "Name of Your Street Drill" and how it applies to your Body Language for the rest of your life.

BODY LANGUAGE

What is this illustration's theme and what could be the hidden message/s in the illustration?

BODY LANGUAGE

Kids, your body language says a lot about you.

It tells the world if you have **confidence or not** in almost everything you do.

If your shoulders are **drooping** and you appear to always be looking at the ground,

A bully will surely see your poor body language, and quickly decide you're the perfect kid to **hound**.

You must stand tall, walk with your chin up and shoulders back. You'll be telling the world you are a kid that is alert and aware.

The bully will take one long look at you and **quickly conclude** you're not someone to be picked on at all. The best choice for the bully will be to go elsewhere.

Be proud of who you are each and every day and **display it from head to toe**.

Your good body language will be a powerful tool for you to use. It may be all you need to **prevent** the bully from coming anywhere close.

Al Johnson

BODY LANGUAGE VOCABULARY: Drooping, hound, conclude, display, prevent

Instructor Introduces: Being Street Smart & How it applies to Bullying:

Do You Know What Being Street Smart Means?

- **Answer:** Most importantly, it means you **being keenly aware of the world around you** always – at school, at play, in the park, with your parents, at the mall, and wherever you go.

Instructor will remind you of the mall scenario, when you were taught the drop, spread eagle, and military crawl—You will be asked to demonstrate.

You will be Reminded of the following stories relating to a GUN being used in a naturally frightening Bullying situation:

    1. 6-year old & 11-year-old brothers playing in an alley

    2. Resident in the neighborhood across from an elementary school firing his rifle on a campus full of children at an elementary school

Instructor will have you Role Play what to do if gunfire breaks out around you, including "Emergency Running Skills."

Parent/Teacher Will Reinforce with You: Anticipating trouble or a possible bully situation before it occurs by being **Mentally Tough** is very important in preventing and eliminating bullying.

- All the above relates to being able to "Think on Your Feet" in an emergency or uncomfortable situation.

Instructor Introduces Street Awareness Scenarios Training

Students: At some point in time, if not already, you will be walking from point A to point B without adult supervision. Bullies can come in all ages, shapes, skin colors, and sizes, looking for the opportunity to take advantage of you.

Keen Street Awareness is a **VITAL LIFE SKILL that You MUST have.** You **DO NOT** have to be looking at your iPhone or any other electronic device constantly when you are in public. By doing so, you are **NOT KEENLY AWARE,** therefore the Bully can easily approach you with the **ELEMENT OF SURPRISE**.

Today's Street Awareness Lesson:

Instructor will now teach The Safer Side of the Street to walk on and why.

- **Instructor Reinforces and Students Role Play: (Video instruction):** Picking up an available **BLUNT OBJECT** (If available) on the street when being followed or threatened by someone with negative intent, and what to do with it. **It is not what you think!** (Options that could be critical in keeping you safe)

- **Instructor Reinforces and Students Role Play: (Video instruction)** Creating an imaginary friendly person or relative on the street. **(You will learn to create "The Element of Surprise" and a "Diversion" when threaten or you are made to feel uncomfortable)**

Instructor Reinforces and Students Role Play: (Video instruction) Blind Spots and Street Safety

Instructor Reinforces and Students Role Play (Video instruction) How you would walk **to your destination, for example, from 20th to 25th Street.** You could be either walking alone or with friends. **Your iPhones and electronic devices come into play:**

Suddenly, out of nowhere, someone appears behind you, instantly making you feel uncomfortable with an aggressive act or enticement.

Instructor/Parent Reminds Students of Previous Story: About how Al Johnson used an enticing and persuasive ruse in a street situation with a 12-year-old boy, he had never seen before, as a test to see how the boy would react to a total stranger.

Instructor/Parent Reinforces How: Awareness, Hitting "The Light Switch," the 3R's, SIC, Mental Toughness, and Body Language all play an important role in these Street Safety Awareness situations and your anti-bullying training.

Instructor Reinforces: What you MUST YELL if you want attention drawn to you in an emergency street situation and why.

The word "FIRE" should be yelled more than the word "HELP"—e.g., fire, fire, fire, fire, help, help, fire.

Instructor/Parent Reminds Students of The Story: About a 17-year-old high school girl who was assaulted by a gang of boys as she walked home from school. How the neighbors responded to her as she was yelling for **HELP** is very important to this lesson on yelling for **HELP!**

BEING STREET-SMART

What is this illustration's theme and what could be the hidden message/s in the illustration?

BEING STREET-SMART

You may be asking yourself, **"What does being street-smart mean and what does that have to do with me?"**

Almost all kids are **sheltered** and **protected** by their parents or other responsible adults, and that's how it should be.

When a bully **hassles** another kid, that kid is no longer under the **protective umbrella** of parents or responsible adults. The kid is left to fend for him/herself all too often, eventually in the **mean streets**.

If a kid is not street-smart, and most are not, **the bully has the advantage.** The bully is then tough to defeat.

Being street-smart is **being confident, alert, aware, and having the ability to create confusion and doubt in the bully's mind.**

This is not easily done when a kid has been sheltered all the time.

Being street-smart is **knowing words to say, things to do, and not do** when a bully has decided he/she wants to bully you.

Being street-smart is doing exactly what a bully doesn't expect you to do.

Bullies carefully avoid street-smart kids, so make sure the bully quickly knows to stay away from you.

Street-smart kids create on the fly, as quickly as can be.

A street-smart kid's antennae are sharply tuned for any negative possibility.

Street-smart kids quickly reverse a bully situation in their favor. A kid must be trained to be street-smart by someone who knows and understands the streets.

It may or may not be the parents who do the training; however, **what a kid wants to avoid, is for the street-smart training to come from the bully.**

Al Johnson

STREET SMART VOCABULARY: Sheltered, protected, protective umbrella, fend, avoid, create on the fly, antennae, sharply tuned

Instructor/Parent Discusses with Students: Words, phrases, and stanzas in bold print for their meanings and overall importance regarding the Theme and Main Idea of the poem.

Instructor/Parent to Students: You have just completed your 4th Lesson in the Bullies Be Gone! Project Training Program. Let's now take a look at how much you have learned from these lessons and, more importantly, how well you have retained the information.

End of Lessons #3 & #4 – No meditation drill for this class (Instructor's Discretion) You should practice the meditation drill on your own at home.

Instructor/Parent to Students: Answer the following questions with your best responses to Al Johnson at the email address previously given. Make sure your responses and answers are yours and not your parent's or teacher's.

Your quiz will be graded by our staff or your parent/teacher, and promptly returned to you. Upon successful completion of the entire Bullies Be Gone Comprehensive Course, you will be awarded a Certificate of Completion, along with a Bonus Gift. **Al Johnson will personally put comments on your quiz to enhance you learning effective skills and techniques to eliminate or prevent bullying.**

Bullies Be Gone Retention Quiz — Lessons 1–4

Your Name: _____ Age_____

1. **Hitting "The Light Switch"** is all about a child's or teen's what?

2. Explain how using the Hitting "The Light Switch" technique could prevent you from being bullied or help eliminate a bullying problem you might have.

3. What are **the 3R's** and in what specific order should they take place?

R_____ R_____ R_____

4. Explain what happens with each of the 3R's and why knowing the proper use of each one could help you prevent being bullied or eliminate a problem you currently may be having with a bully.

R

R

R

5. What does it mean to be **Mentally Tough** and why is it important for a child/teen to have Mental Toughness to defeat the bully or prevent being bullied. And to be mentally tough, no matter what age a person happens to be?

6. Children and Teens who are keenly _____ and know how bullies act and carry themselves stand a much better chance of not being bullied. (Fill in the blank with the correct word to complete the statement.)

Why did you answer the way you did in #6? Explain in the space below:

7. What does **Good Body Language** have to do with keeping a bully or bad person away from you and how you appear to the world around you?

8. How would you describe good body language? How would you describe poor or bad body language?

Good Body Language

Poor or Bad Body Language

9. What message(s) do you get from the **Awareness Illustration**? & What is the theme or main idea of the poem?

10. What message(s) do you get from the **Body Language Illustration?** & What is the theme or main idea of the Body Language poem?

Children, teens, and adults should test their knowledge of the first 4 lessons by taking the quiz. There will be 10 points given for each correct response for a total of 100 points.

Partially correct answers get 5 points and incorrect answers get zero points. **Any total score less than 75** requires going back and re-studying lessons 1–4 and retest.

Learning and Retaining the **BBGP Vital Life Skills Training** of each lesson is mandatory for you. By doing so, you will develop skills and techniques that give you the best chance to **Effectively Eliminate or Prevent Bullying via Self-Empowerment!**

Lessons 5-6 — For BBGP Instructors, Parents, Teachers, Children & Teens — Cyberspace Bullying — A Real Epidemic in Our Society

Instructor/Parent Will: Discuss any events that occurred with you since the last class that involved Bullying. If this occurred, you will share with the entire class or parent. (Could be something you were involved in or ones you observed)

- Physical Fitness Training
- Instructor Will Review Important Previous Lessons

Instructor/Parents to Students: The following important lessons are designed to help you learn effective methods of offsetting, deflecting, nullifying the effects of, and rendering insignificant to you:

THE BULLY'S HATEFUL WORDS & NASTY RUMORS online that may be directed toward you or a close friend.

You will now begin to understand ways to develop Skills, Techniques, and **POWERFUL WORDS** to defeat the online bully's inappropriate intent.

You will learn to do this with **EMPOWERING CONFIDENCE & CONVICTION.** The six Poetic and Powerful lessons your instructor will cover are:

Hateful Words, Rumors Online, You Hide In Front Of a Computer, Social Skills Too, Social Network Caution & The Stranger On The Internet

"**WORDS CAN:** Deflate, Harm, Hurt & Kill"

"**WORDS CAN:** Empower, Build Self-Confidence, Inspire & Heal"

The latter are exactly what WORDS in the Bullies Be Gone! Project are designed to do.

If you understand:
- Specific Words to say
- How to say them (Effectively with Conviction)
- When and When not to say them
- What actions to take after saying them
- When and how to say them

You will be in a stronger position to not allow rumors online to negatively affect your self-confidence and self-esteem.

You will begin to know or improve knowing the importance of who you really are as a person and the self-pride you should always display, no matter what anyone says negatively about you. YOU MUST BELIEVE THIS WITH CONVICTION! By doing so, YOU'LL BECOME MORE SELF-EMPOWERED!

- Your Parent/Teacher will read the following powerful message. You will be instructed to read along:

"IT'S NOT WHAT A BULLY SAYS ABOUT YOU ONLINE, NO MATTER HOW HATEFUL OR NASTY IT IS. WHAT DETERMINES THE FINAL OUTCOME IS HOW YOU ALLOW WHAT IS SAID TO AFFECT WHO YOU REALLY ARE! NO ONE HAS THE VERBAL POWER TO MAKE YOU FEEL DEFEATED, INSIGNIFICANT, SAD, OR WEAK, UNLESS YOU ALLOW THEM TO HAVE IT! YOUR MENTAL TOUGHNESS IS MUCH MORE POWERFUL THAN THE BULLY'S MENTAL WEAKNESS!" **Remember these WORDS for the rest of your wonderful life!**

Instructor/Parent to Students: Always Remember:

You must remind yourself of the following over and over again, and have it ingrained in your Mental Toughness Mind:

MY DIFFERENCE IS MY STRENGTH! Refer to the poem and illustration" My Difference Is My Strength" in this course and study and learn the important words, phrases, stanzas, and the poem itself for the enhancement of your **Self-Empowerment!**

These techniques and **WORDS** if learned well, practiced, and retained, will give you a much better chance of successfully Eliminating and Preventing cyberspace bullying.

Parent/Teacher Continues and Reminds Students:

Specific phrases, stanzas, and WORDS in your training, also send powerful messages to bullies to cease their inappropriate behavior.

Parent/Teacher will Reinforce:
As you read and study the poems, you should make believe you are talking directly to the bully with POWERFUL WORDS in the poem. Looking the bully in the eye, belief in what you are saying with conviction, mental toughness, voice inflection, and confidence, are all paramount for effectiveness.

This role-playing scenario should be done, even when you are copying and pasting specific phrases or stanzas as a response to the bully online. As you are doing so, your tablet, computer, laptop, etc. actually becomes the bully. **LOOK THE BULLY IN THE EYE WHILE PASTING!**

Your online response to the bully will be **unique, surprising, and unexpected. Surprise and Confusion** almost always deflates or defeat's a bully's intent, mentally and physically, especially mentally!

Instructor Reinforces with Students: It is highly important for you to clearly understand the main idea or theme of each poem and the same for the illustration, including any hidden message(s) in the illustration.

Compare your point of view with your parent's/teacher's point of view of the main idea and theme of each poem and illustration. Everyone learns with this interaction and open dialogue.

Parent/Teacher Reinforces: Study the illustration of each poem carefully before and after you read the poem. Look for hidden message/s in each illustration. What is the illustration saying to the student and what does it say to the parents/teacher?

Enjoy learning the skills and techniques in the Bullies Be Gone! Project. You will acquire knowledge currently **95% of all children and teens, no matter their place of residence, DO NOT POSSESS KNOWLEDGE OF.**

Instructor Reinforces with Students: In some poems, **WORDS** of the poem and stanzas will be speaking directly to you, to build your self-confidence and self-esteem. In other poems, the **WORDS** are speaking to the bully, strongly suggesting he/she immediately cease their inappropriate behavior! Other poems will be speaking to you and the Bully. Some poems even speak to your parents and teachers.

Read the poems numerous times, each time with more **determination** and **conviction** to not be a victim of bullying ever again or not at all.

You **MUST EMPOWER** yourself with words that make you feel strong and the bully appear to you and to him or herself as being weak and insignificant.

Parent/Teacher Will Take a Survey Requiring Your Participation:

HATEFUL WORDS

What is this illustration's theme and what could be the hidden message/s in the illustration?

HATEFUL WORDS

Do you have any idea how much hateful words hurt those kids you're **spewing** them out to?

If you're a bully who uses them, you need to know **they hurt deeply** and could scar a kid for life. Is that what you really want to do?

It may seem like **innocent fun** when you're bullying other kids. The truth is it's not!

If you're a bully, because of the **negative impact** you can have on another kid, you must immediately stop!

I once thought bullying was cool, too, so I would say hateful words to other kids, just to see how they would react.

I would say hateful words to their face. I would say them behind their back.

Then, out of nowhere, I heard the same kind of hateful words, meant for me.

I didn't like it a bit; in fact, I was hurt and angry as can be.

So, I immediately stopped using hateful words. I'm so glad I did.

No one **deserves** to hear hateful words, especially coming from another kid.

Al Johnson

HATEFUL WORDS VOCABULARY: Spewing, hurt deeply, innocent fun, negative impact, deserves

Rumors Online

What is this illustration's theme and what could be the hidden message/s in the illustration?

RUMORS ONLINE

The rumors online about me, coming from you, are lies and you know it.

Are you spreading rumors because you're really jealous of me and this is how you've chosen to show it?

Come on! Is spreading **vicious**, stupid rumors the best you can do?

You're trying to destroy me, but the truth is, in the end, your lies are going to destroy you.

If your intent was to make me feel bad about myself, with rumors spreading all over the Internet,

Congratulations, you **initially succeeded**, but I refuse to go into a **shell-of-shame** because of you. I now **declare** your rumors **meaningless** at best.

You see, my parents and others that care about me have helped me find my **inner strength** that was stuck in quicksand.

I looked in the mirror one day and decided no one can destroy me unless I allow him or her the ability to. Moreover, I should be quite proud of who I am.

So, I strongly suggest you **cease** spreading your rumors and lies about me or anyone else throughout cyberspace.

Your rumors online have no clout anymore. I declare them **baseless** and empty threats. In the real world of decent, good, and respectful people where I live, your rumors have no place.

Al Johnson

RUMORS ONLINE VOCABULARY: Vicious, intent, initially succeeded, meaningless, shell-of-shame, declare, inner strength, cease, clout, baseless

You Hide In Front Of A Computer

What is this illustration's theme and what could be the hidden message/s in the illustration?

YOU HIDE IN FRONT OF A COMPUTER

You're a bully that hides in front of a computer sending out messages of lies, **disrespect**, and hate.

If you must hide in front of a computer to bully me, you're not the **least bit brave** at all. In fact, you're a **phony** and a **fake**.

I actually feel sorry for you as you **hopelessly linger** in your **pathetic state**.

The truth about me or any kid you're bullying will eventually come out. Truth is frightening for you, isn't it? Because **the truth will seal your fate**.

You hide in front of a computer for hours at a time.

Your time would be better spent if somehow you discovered, with other kids, you could become nice and kind.

You hide in front of a computer to go about your **daily sour routine** of bullying other kids.

One day your computer will crash and along with it, your **despicable bullying empire**, too. Just maybe then, you'll feel somewhat sorry for all the **unnecessary** bullying you did.

Al Johnson

YOU HIDE IN FRONT OF A COMPUTER VOCABULARY: Disrespect, least bit brave, phony, fake, hopelessly linger, pathetic state, seal your fate, daily sour routine, despicable, unnecessary

SOCIAL SKILLS TOO

What is this illustration's theme and what could be the hidden message/s in the illustration?

SOCIAL SKILLS TOO

Kids primarily learn academic skills in school.

However, we must teach kids social skills, too.

Kids learn lots of social skills from caring and loving parents as they grow.

Kids need to build on social skills taught in the home. There are real world social skills, too, they must know.

When a kid decides to bully other kids, it is obvious that he/she lacks social skills.

Even if kids aren't bullies, but use profanity and foul language a lot, as so many do, they are lacking social skills.

If a kid is disrespectful to parents, teachers, and other adults, they lack social skills.

It's apparent a kid would not become a bully if he/she had proper social skills.

Learning math, English, reading, writing, and science are all important vital subjects that kids must learn and do.

However, it is just as important for kids to be taught and acquire proper social skills, too.

Al Johnson

SOCIAL SKILLS VOCABULARY: Primarily, obvious, lacks, profanity, foul language, acquire

SOCIAL NETWORK CAUTION

What is this illustration's theme and what could be the hidden message/s in the illustration?

SOCIAL NETWORK CAUTION

Social networks on the Internet are popular with kids, especially teens.

Responsible parents put a block on anything online their children should not hear or see.

Kids you may not like the block, but it's being done because your parents want to protect you.

If you find a way around the block, accessing social networks, be responsible; avoid doing anything online your parents have instructed you not to do.

You'll be **showing respect** for your parents, yourself, and **tremendous restraint**, strength, and **wisdom**, because you may have been **tempted** to.

For teens especially, if you're allowed to go on social networks, **heed your parents' instructions.** People are always online looking to take advantage of a teen like you.

Do not hold conversations in "chat rooms" with anyone you initially meet online. To do so is one of the most dangerous things you can do.

If someone online offers to meet you in person, there are no ifs, ands, or buts to consider; telling your parents immediately is what you must do!

Many kids have been taken advantage of by people they've met online.

Always use social network caution skills when you are online. If you do so, you will be a kid who will successfully make it through your youthful years safe, sound, and absolutely, just fine.

Al Johnson

SOCIAL NETWORK CAUTION VOCABULARY: Responsible, accessing, tremendous restraint, wisdom, tempted, heed, initially, immediately, sound

THE STRANGER ON THE INTERNET

What is this illustration's theme and what could be the hidden message/s in the illustration?

THE STRANGER ON THE INTERNET

The stranger on the internet should be treated just like the stranger on the street.

Parents and responsible adults have told their children never talk to strangers they might meet.

The stranger on the Internet is **constantly on the prowl, looking for any kid they can convince.**

The stranger on the internet knows **slick and enticing ways** to cause a kid to let down his/her defense.

Kids, if you ever come across a stranger on the Internet,

Do not, under any circumstance, chat with them. Conversations with strangers on the Internet can only lead to regret.

Quickly tell your parents or any **responsible adult** about the stranger on the Internet.

Hopefully, you can do this while the stranger is still online.

Then, if the stranger is a bad person that commits crimes against kids, maybe the police can catch him/her quickly. They will then be the stranger on the Internet hopefully, for the very last time.

Al Johnson

STRANGER ON THE INTERNET VOCABULARY: Constantly on the prowl, convince, enticing, regret, responsible adult

Lessons 5-6 Scenario: Students, you have responded to this scenario before, however, we want to see if your BBGP training will induce different responses to the same or similar occurrence.

Instructor to Students: This scenario could happen to you at any time online and when you least expect it — (Use for homework for the class)

To your surprise, one day when you go to school, everyone is looking at you in a strange way, even pointing fingers and laughing at you. You have no clue as to what is going on. This has never happened to you before and the situation is making you feel very uncomfortable. You soon find out the rumors are coming from postings on the Internet on Social Media sites.

To make it more troubling, the rumors are coming from someone you know. You are aware that rumors on the Internet could be seen, read, and heard by thousands of people. This, of course, makes you feel even worse.

Before you answer the following, I want you to be totally truthful as to how you would react to the questions below:

Email your responses to the scenario above to Al Johnson. Make sure your parents are aware that you are emailing. Get your parents involved; however, your final answers must be yours and not your parents or teachers.

Your Name_____ Age_____

Respond with your answers to the following questions pertaining to the Scenario above:

A. How would you handle the situation above if it happened to you or how did you handle it, if it, or if something similar has ever happened to you?

B. What would you specifically say to the person spreading the rumors, if anything, since you may know him/her personally? Would you respond face to face with the person or online or both ways? (Hint: Especially now that you have had lessons in Bullies Be Gone! Project training)

C. If you know the rumors are not true, which they more than likely aren't, would it bother you at all because of knowing it's false information? Why would it bother you? Or why would it not bother you?

D. If the situation was happening to a close friend of yours, would you get involved to help your friend? Yes? No? If Yes, how would you get involved? If No, why would you not get involved?

E. How would you truly feel with this scenario happening to you? Be candid and state exactly what you believe your initial response would be. Would your response be different now, if it ever happened, because of your new Bullies Be Gone! Project knowledge?

Instructor to Students: Please be very truthful with your responses to the questions, no matter what your answers are. Do not be ashamed of how you might think you would feel with the scenario above happening to you.

When your responses are received by BBGP staff, a critique by Al Johnson will be emailed back to you. The learning process should be FUN. Our goal is to give you vital life skills training that 95% of all children and teens DO NOT possess knowledge of. And to empower you to eliminate or prevent online bullying!

Learning, practicing, and retaining the Vital Life Skills Training of BBGP lessons are mandatory for a child or teen to successfully Eliminate or Prevent a bullying problem.

Instructor to Students: Learning and retaining the Vital Life Skills Training of each lesson is mandatory to help you **prevent** or **eliminate** a bullying problem.

Meditation Drill — Instructor/Parent Discretion

Instructor Reminds Students: The proper way to practice, study, and train, for best results from The Bullies Be Gone! Project Training.

Instructor Will Go Over Next Week's Training:
Mental & Physical Self-Defense Training (Escaping & Controlling Purposes Only)
Cyberspace Anti-Bullying Training (Role Playing Continued)

Email your scenario responses to: Al Johnson @ al@antibullyingexpert.com

END OF LESSONS #5 & #6

Lessons #6 & #7 – For BBGP Instructors, Parents, Teachers, Children & Teens (This will be a continuation of Lessons #5 & #6)

- Continuation of Cyberspace Bullying
- Introduction of Mental & Physical Self-Defense (For Controlling & Escaping Only)
- Physical Fitness Warm up Exercises (approx. 10-15 minutes)
- Role Playing Scenario for Class & Homework

Instructor Reinforces and Reviews: Awareness, Hitting "The Light Switch," The 3R's, Mental Toughness, SIC, Body Language, Being Street Smart, Hateful Words, Rumors Online, You Hide In Front Of A Computer, Social Skills Too, Social Network Caution & The Stranger On The Internet. **It is Critical you learn and retain these skills to prevent and protect against bullying.**

Students, you will again share any occurrences during the week since the last class that required the use of your BBGP skills. Did you witness or were involved in any Bullying situations or potential ones? If there were incidents, discussions should take place with instructor/parent and the entire class. (If applicable)

BASIC SELF-DEFENSE – It is not necessary to study self-defense for many years, unless one chooses. However, in today's society, learning basic self-defense techniques that could prevent you or your family from becoming easy **victims**, is a very wise decision to undertake.

Knowledge of simple, **BUT EFFECTIVE** self-defense techniques applicable to **THE STREETS should be knowledge for the entire family.** In BBGP training, these skills are to be used for **Controlling or Escaping** purposes ONLY.

In the following lesson, **Martial Arts Master Al Johnson** will teach you the all-important first steps of applying BASIC SELF-DEFENSE in a PRACTICAL manner. The training is REAL WORLD SELF-DEFENSE, NOT SPORT ORIENTED.

Learn and practice the following and you will be off to a good start in acquiring **PRACTICAL STREET SELF-DEFENSE SKILLS:**

Lesson #1 – Physical Self-Defense (Video Training)

Students, you MUST clearly understand the following:
Mental Self-Defense is always a vital component of Physical self-defense (Instructor will explain as necessary)

Instructor/Parents to Students:

What you are about to learn is Physical Self-Defense skills for **Escape** and **Controlling** purposes ONLY.

INSTRUCTOR WILL EMPHASIZE: Fighting is **NEVER** the first choice in the Bullies Be Gone! Project training for **Eliminating** or **Preventing** a bullying problem.

However, 99.9 percent of the time when a child or teen is being physically bullied, there is **NO ADULT** on the scene. The adult shows up after the fact. **A push, shove, aggressive grab, or punch to an innocent child/teen can occur within a split second, and almost always does.**

Instructor to Students: It is important you learn and acquire effective ways to escape from or control an aggressive physical encounter with a bully, until a **responsible adult** is on the scene or contacted in some way. (For example, look at the aggressive encounter on the front cover of your workbook) You will be taught effective methods to defend yourself from this type of aggression and others.

You are to apply these skills **ONLY** after being trained and when you are left with no other choice **(including running or walking away)** because of a bully's physical aggression. Sometimes the best Self-Defense skill may be to RUN away from the bully with the **"Emergency Running Skills"** you have been taught in this training.

Introduction to Self-Defense by Instructor/Parent:

The following mathematical formula of **Physics** applies to **Physical Self-Defense** in a major way:

Instructor/Parent Explains To Students: Mass x Acceleration = Force (Instructor Demonstration)

Knowing the way this formula applies to the Human Body and the delivery of Self-Defense Techniques is Critical – Let's break the formula down:

Mass is a person's body weight that can be **increased** at the **moment of delivery (Impact)** of a self-defense technique, if a person knows how to do so.

Acceleration is the speed in which the self-defense technique is delivered.

Force is the **impact** of the delivery of the technique.

Objective: Effectively increase your Body Mass, Speed & Force for maximum effect when delivering a self-defense technique.

For example: Two cars are heading straight toward each other at 35 miles per hour and a head-on collision occurs:

Mass = The weight **(Mass)** of the car x **Acceleration** (35 miles an hour) **Speed** of the car = **Force** = collision, damage at impact

More damage is increased at impact by simply **increasing the speed to 50 miles** an hour or more. (Or if the vehicle is a heavier one)

Results = More damage at impact.

The formula is **VERY IMPORTANT and KEY** to generating maximum effectiveness when applying **SELF-DEFENSE TECHNIQUES.**

This result of FORCE is exactly why physical self-defense in the BBGP program is used ONLY AS A LAST RESORT in a physically threatening bullying encounter. In addition, we DO NOT want children and teens fighting at school, or anywhere else.

You must know specific techniques to use against an attacker, if you have no other choice. The skills we teach are designed for you to use quickly, **retreat and seek adult help. Awareness, Hitting "The Light Switch, The 3R's, and SIC** all apply in the effective use of physical self-defense for Escape and Controlling purposes ONLY!

By you possessing this knowledge, hopefully, the ELEMENT OF SURPRISE will be created, giving you the window needed to control or escape a physical attack by a Bully.

How to Apply the Formula of Physics with the Human Body:

Mass x Acceleration = Force

USE OF THE HIP APPLICATION

Practice the following to begin learning how THE USE OF THE HIP WORKS – Applying specific self-defense techniques by the Use of The Hips will be taught.

In almost every major sport, proper Use of The Hip is Applied:

- Boxing
- Tennis
- Golf
- Baseball
- Football
- Martial Arts (MMA, Judo, or Karate schools where the Use of The Hip is a MAJOR component of training — All Martial Arts DO NOT emphasis the proper use of the hip)
- Wrestling
- Hockey

There are others, the above mentioned are obvious — you will understand better after you practice the following exercise:

Learning to Apply the Use of The Hips: (Video demonstration)

There is a Long Hip & a Short Hip — Both are effective and used in delivering self-defense techniques depending on the distance from the person you are striking to defend yourself.

In the following example of using the hip, you'll be using the **Long Hip — The person is within arm's length of you or can be with a quick distance adjustment on your part:**

- Stand with your knees slightly bent, your feet about shoulder-width apart, no wider, and your toes pointed inward. (Not in a pigeon-toed position or in a tense manner)

- Make sure you are relaxed, take a deep breath. **(Inhale — Take the air in through your nose)**, and quickly release the breath **(Exhale — blow the air out through your mouth)** — You can do this a few times until you feel totally relaxed. Remember the earlier relaxation exercises taught in your BBGP Training.

- Slightly bend your knees, they must not be locked — you are in a position similar to sitting in the saddle of a horse — the bending of the knees and sitting in the saddle gives you better balance and proper use of your legs.

(Your Legs are your Foundation) You will hear the following statement often by announcers of the sport of Boxing:

The fighters need to sit down on their punches to develop the necessary power. They are standing too upright.

- Your legs play a very important role in the Use of The Hips.
- Don't worry about what you are going to do with your hands (Technique-wise) at this time. However, a good habit to form with your hands from the beginning is to **keep your hands high** at mid-face level, just inside your shoulders, with elbows in, not extended out like wings.
- Make sure your hands are at least the same level of a physically threatening bully in front of you, preferably, your hands are up in a non-intimidating manner, and slightly higher than the bully's hands. (Instructor will demonstrate)

Keep your hands in this area while practicing the use of the hip. This also helps you form the habit of keeping your hands up in a possible close, aggressive, physical encounter with someone who could be throwing a punch at you. A punch by a bully could be thrown at the same time you are delivering a self-defense technique to control or escape. **(An effective protection technique of your head and face from a punch or blunt object will be taught in your self-defense training.)**

Now imagine that you are preparing to strike a target directly in front of you. (A person that you now must defend yourself against) Specific striking techniques will be taught in your BBGP training. **The key here is to keep your eyes glued to the target even while your hips are rotating.** (Never lose sight of the target or eye contact — you should be able to do both). (Instructor will demonstrate.)

Now quickly pivot on the balls of the feet to your left at an angle of about 45 degrees. Then quickly return to the original position you started from. Repeat the same process a multitude of times.

Your body position when you pivot should be:
- Feet and belly button at a 45-degree angle, right shoulder should be pointing toward the bully you are striking and left shoulder should be at a 90-degree angle. **You have just practiced the use of the right hip.**

- Remember, your eyes remain glued to the target you are striking and to the bully's eyes always. Practice on the opposite side also, so that you are using the left hip, everything is the same, but in the opposite direction.

You can also know if your hip is moving properly or not by placing a finger on your BELLY BUTTON before you pivot 45 degrees. If your belly button does not move to a 45-degree angle as described above, you did not pivot and use your hip correctly.

- Begin pivoting faster and faster until the process becomes natural. All the points mentioned above must be in play as you are pivoting your hips.
- Practice properly does not mean to do the drill a few times and quit. It MUST be done hundreds and hundreds, and hundreds of times, (Over a period of time) until you lose count — then start practicing all over again.
- Once you master pivoting on one side, quickly switch and pivot on the opposite side — rotate over and over again on both sides.
- Don't forget where your hands are, they are up at face level all the time you are rotating your hip and your eyes never leave the target you will be striking. (Unless you have one hand with a finger on the BELLY BUTTON at the beginning of your training — Instructor will demonstrate)
- **You ARE NOT yet delivering a self-defense technique.** You are learning how to use and rotate your hip properly, so it becomes natural when you do begin delivering self-defense techniques.

Short Hip application will be easier, once you master the use of the Long Hip

Results of proper Use of the Hip above: Mass x Acceleration = Force

For example: Your natural body weight is = 150lbs = **Mass** (Your body **Mass**)
The faster you pivot your Hip **Coupled** with the **Speed** of the technique = Increased **Acceleration**

Results: Powerful Impact = Force

What will transpire is without you consciously having to think about the proper Use of the Hip: Upon impact, your weight is temporarily increased. (By at least 10% upon Impact) **Results:** The self-defense technique you deliver immediately becomes more devastating. (This is why Fighting IS NEVER a 1st response to a Bully)

Practice over and over again until the **Use of The Hip is automatic**. When the application of self-defense techniques are coupled with hip rotation, you will begin developing Effective and Powerful Skills for Controlling and Escaping purposes ONLY!

Physical Self-Defense Techniques: (Video demonstration)

- Instructor will Teach & Reinforce "Emergency Running Skills" (Video demonstration & Role Playing)
- Shoulder Spin
- Shoulder grab from behind
- Escaping from Wall Pin or Tree Pin Situation (Mainly applies to girls/ladies)
- Adams Apple Pinch
- Self-Defense against a punch or blunt instrument strike (Supported Elbow Frame protecting the face and head)
- Spear Hand & Reverse Spear Hand
- Claw Hand & Reverse Claw Hand
- Wrist Grabs (Single, Front & Behind) Straight Across, Cross, Double from Front & Behind
- Single & Double Lapel grab
- Sleeve Grabs
- Headlock Defense (Pressure points & more)
- Bear Hug Defense (Around the arms & Between the arms)
- Two Hand Choke (In front & behind)
- Rear Naked Choke (The dangers of)
- Arm Bar Technique
- Foot Stomp Technique & Shin Kick
- Aikido Techniques & Footwork

Student Homework Scenario: (Instructor will give details)

The Scenario: *You are in team competition or a lively practice session on the soccer field, basketball court, baseball diamond, or football field and during the action, you get hit in the knee, and you crumble to the ground in pain. A kid unexpectedly comes up to you and calls you a "**Wimp**," (**Or any other name to make you feel as if you are a "cry baby"**) because you are holding your knee in pain, unable to stand up. The kid laughs at you and calls you "Wimp" again. Some of the other kids begin to laugh at you also.*

Before you answer the following, I want you to be totally truthful as to **how you believe you would react according to the questions below.**

I want you to email me your responses to the scenario above, with your name and age or bring your responses to the next class session for your parent/teacher to evaluate (If applicable). Make sure your parents know you are emailing me. Get your parents involved, but your answers must be your answers, not your parents.

I want you to tell me:

- How would you handle the scene above if it happened to you?

- What would you say to the kid who called you a "Wimp," if anything?

- Would it even bother you the least bit if a kid called you a "Wimp" under the circumstances with your painful knee? Why would it bother you? Why would it not bother you?

- Would you be concerned about how your peers and friends react to the situation, since they probably heard the "Wimp" reference and witnessed your reaction. Some kids laughed at you or heard about it later in a gossiping moment? If so, why? If not, why not?

- Has anything similar to this ever happened to you? If so, how did you react then? Would you react differently now? If so, how? If not, why not? **(Hint: Your BBGP training may come into play)**

Students: For me or your instructor/parent to help empower you, please be very truthful, no matter your response. Do not be ashamed of how you might think you would feel with the scene above happening to you. When Al Johnson receives your responses to the questions, he will email back to you a critique. **The goal is to give you skills and techniques that 95% of all children and teens DO NOT have knowledge of.**

Learning and Retaining the Vital Life Skills Training of each lesson is mandatory for you in order to successfully **Eliminate** or **Prevent** a bullying problem.

No Meditation Drill for this week's lesson (Instructor discretion)

Instructor/Parent will go over next week's training:

Self-Defense, Scenarios, Cyberspace bullying continued, Role Playing & Additional Educational Poetic Instruction

E-mail your responses to: Al Johnson @ al@antibullyexpert.com

END OF LESSONS #6 & #7

If you are emailing your responses to Al, make sure your parents are aware that you are doing so.

Your name_____Age_____

Your Email address _____

Lesson #8 — For BBG Instructors, Parents, Children & Teens

Your Instructor/Parent will:

- Discuss any events where bullying came into play that you were directly involved in or witnessed
- Review previous lessons in your BBGP training

Physical Fitness Warm Up

Self-Defense Training Continued (Techniques covered will depend on last week's training and students grasp and retention of skills taught)

Instructor to Students: The following important lessons are designed to help you learn effective methods and WORDS to offset hateful and disrespectful WORDS by bullies. In addition, these lessons will help enhance your understanding of effective methods to use if it becomes necessary to stand up to the bully with confidence and conviction, and how to apply them.

Poems of Empowerment, Inspiration, Motivation & Training in this lesson are: Your Nasty Words Cannot Hurt Me, You Tried To Defeat Me, I Will Not Be Your Victim Anymore & My Difference Is My Strength.

"WORDS can Deflate, Harm, Hurt, and Kill!"

"WORDS can Empower, Build Self-Confidence, Inspire, and Heal."

If you are **Keenly Aware** of your environment, combined with **Being Street Smart**, these skills alone could be sufficient enough to cause a bully to seek an easier victim, or maybe cause the bully to self-reflect, and cease bullying altogether.

These techniques, if learned well and retained, will give you a much better chance of **Eliminating and Preventing** a bullying problem.

Students: It is important you are consistent with the following for your Bullies Be Gone! Project training to be effective against a bully.

- Study and memorize words, stanzas, and specific poems for your overall empowerment and the bully's overall weakness.
- Each poem contains WORDS, PHRASES & STANZAS to empower you and off-

set the effects of a bully's nasty words and negative intent.

- Make sure you understand the Main Idea or Theme of each poem and illustration, and look for any hidden messages in the illustration.
- Discuss the poem with your parents and teachers.
- Express your point of view of the poem and illustration, ask your instructor/parent to express theirs.
- Study the illustration of each poem carefully before and after you read the poem.

You should enjoy learning skills and techniques to help you develop effective ways of **Eliminating** or **Preventing** a bullying problem permanently.

For this to occur, you must learn, practice, and retain the messages sent with these poetic **words according to the BBGP Training Recommendations. Your Self-Empowerment is our goal!**

As you read the poems, make believe you are talking directly to the bully with the words in the poem. If you ever must say them face to face to a bully, I want you to develop the confidence to do so, if you don't have it now.

If your confidence is currently strong, I want the **words** you learn in all the Bullies Be Gone! Project lessons to make you even **mentally tougher and more confident**.

If the bullying is occurring online, you can cut and paste powerful poetic response(s) to a bully by using specific powerful lines in the poem that apply to your online bullying situation. Suggestion: 1-4 stanzas copied and pasted at a time will be more effective than pasting the entire poem.

In some poems, the words of the poem will be speaking directly to you, to build your self-confidence and self-esteem. Read the poems a number of times, each time with more **determination** and **conviction** to not be a victim of bullying ever again or not at all. You must empower yourself with words that make you feel strong and the bully appear to you, and hopefully, to himself/herself, as being insignificant and weak.

Some poems will be speaking directly to the bully sending powerful messages to the bully to immediately cease their inappropriate behavior.

As before, your parent/teacher will read the poem out loud, while you follow along silently in your training workbook. When you are asked to read or perform the poem in front of the class, at home or alone, remember to do so with: **Conviction, Belief, Voice Inflection, Determination, and Passion**. You are learning **Effective** ways to **Eliminate & Prevent Bullying!**

YOUR NASTY WORDS CANNOT HURT ME

What is this illustration's theme and what could be the hidden message/s in the illustration?

YOUR NASTY WORDS CANNOT HURT ME

You hoped the nasty words you said to me would hurt so much that, like a turtle, I would go into a permanent shell.

My parents told me not to give a bully that kind of satisfaction. From all the nasty words you said, guess what? I'm not feeling bad at all. In fact, I'm doing quite well.

Yes, your nasty words hurt me at first, just as you wanted them to.

I'm lucky to have parents, responsible adults, and even other kids, who showed me how to defeat bullies like you.

I don't care the **least bit** what you do anymore. I really don't care what you say.

Your nasty words cannot hurt me again. You tried putting me down, but with **self-determination** and help from others, I've been lifted in every way.

I see you as a **small-minded bully**, with no positive direction.

I also see you as a kid who could be nice and kind to others, if you decide to change your **intentions**.

Just in case you **refuse** to change and continue with your bullying ways, **declaring** that's just how it's going to be,

I'm going to do all I can to **spread** my knowledge to as many kids as I can. Then the next kid you try to bully, hopefully, will confidently say to you, "Your nasty words cannot hurt me."

Al Johnson

YOUR NASTY WORDS CANNOT HURT ME VOCABULARY: Least, self-determination, small-minded, intentions, refuse, declaring, spread

I Will Not Be Your Victim Anymore

What is this illustration's theme and what could be the hidden message/s in the illustration?

I WILL NOT BE YOUR VICTIM ANYMORE

I will not be your victim anymore, you've gone too far with your disrespect. I've had enough.

You've bullied me, made me cry, and made me sad and mad, too. You enjoy bullying and stuff.

Suddenly, when I woke up this morning, I decided I will not be your victim anymore.

I was surprised how strong I felt just saying those words to myself repeatedly as I walked out my front door.

"I will not be your victim anymore" are words that have a lot of power if kids who are being bullied truly believe.

If kids repeat, "I will not be your victim anymore," it could give a kid the determination they need to stop the bullying.

Those words sure gave me strength and confidence; they could do the same for you.

No kid deserves to ever be bullied. If you're a kid and you're being bullied, here's what I suggest you do:

Decide that you're no longer going to be bullied like before.

Say these words repeatedly to yourself, then say them to the bully with conviction, when you feel strong and confident: "I will not be your victim anymore!"

Al Johnson

I WILL NOT BE YOUR VICTIM ANYMORE VOCABULARY: Disrespect, determination, decision, conviction, confident

You Tried To Defeat Me

What is this illustration's theme and what could be the hidden message/s in the illustration?

YOU TRIED TO DEFEAT ME

You tried to defeat me with the nasty words you say constantly.

But, instead of your nasty words tearing me down, they lifted me up so I could clearly see.

You're just a lonely bully without any real true friends.

Kids that do hang around with you are just as pathetic, too. I suggest you all find a way for your bullying to end.

You tried to defeat me and probably other kids, too.

For a while, you were successful because I was afraid of you.

But my parents and other responsible adults told me to be confident and strong, no matter how hard it was to be.

They told me this over and over again. One day I was suddenly convinced bullies must prey on weak kids to succeed.

I don't feel weak anymore. In fact, I'm feeling very strong.

You tried to defeat me, it didn't work. From this point on, you had better leave me alone!

Al Johnson

YOU TRIED TO DEFEAT ME VOCABULARY: Constantly, lifted, tearing, pathetic, convinced, prey, succeed

MY DIFFERENCE IS MY STRENGTH

What is this illustration's theme and what could be the hidden message/s in the illustration?

MY DIFFERENCE IS MY STRENGTH

The **difference** in the way I look, walk, talk, or what I **prefer** in life is not my weakness. Because of your **misguided** and **intolerant beliefs**, you need to know, my difference is my strength.

I'm not **ashamed** of who I am. No matter how many nasty things you say about me, my head will be held very high. **My difference is my strength**.

Unfortunately, you must live with your i**gnorance and hate**. Unless you change, you'll carry that heavy **burden** for the rest of your **miserable** life.

That heavy load will eventually wear you down. You'll be stuck in quicksand, slowly sinking, as time rapidly passes you by.

You'll never be the good and **kindhearted** person you could have been. You'll never experience the **brilliance of humankind**.

My difference is my strength. I'm happy with and proud of who I am. My strength lies in my heart and mind.

Your **needless criticism** of me and others too, for no **viable** reason, shows how **shallow** a person you really are.

My difference is my strength. Do you even have the **slightest clue** that your nasty tone **unnecessarily**, goes way too far?

My difference is my strength. Your weakness lies in the disrespectful things you say and do.

My difference is my strength. However, you're not a lost cause. I truly believe there's still a **sliver** of hope for positive change, **longing** to come out, somewhere deep inside you!

If somehow, you haven't clearly understood the powerful message to you I've sent.

Emphatically, I say to you again, my difference is my strength!
MY DIFFERENCE IS MY STRENGTH!!

Al Johnson

MY DIFFERENCE IS MY STRENGTH VOCABULARY: Difference, prefer, misguided, intolerant, ashamed, ignorance, burden, miserable, kindhearted, brilliance, humankind, needless, criticism, viable, shallow, slightest, unnecessarily, sliver of hope, emphatically

INSTRUCTOR SUMMARIZES: THE 8-WEEK COURSE WITH STUDENTS

Instructor Reminds Students: You have learned Vital Life Skills that you should practice and retain for the rest of your life.

What you have learned should never be played with or shown to friends who have not taken this course, with the exception mentioned in earlier lessons.

You should continue to review your training workbook and any other BBGP materials at least once a week, if not more for your retention. Practice you skills at least twice-weekly.

You have successfully completed the 8-week training. You and your instructor/parents have access to Al Johnson and any BBGP instructor for any follow-up questions or concerns @ the following:

al@antibullyingexpert.com
www.antibullyingexpert.com
www.bulliesbegoneproject.com

- **Students** if you have any questions, do not hesitate to ask your parent/teacher.

- To contact Al Johnson directly, consult with parent/teacher first. Al Johnson WILL NOT speak with you without parent permission.

Students should frequently refer to his/her workbook to insure retention of all skills taught.

You have now completed the Bullies Be Gone! Project 8-Week Comprehensive Training: CONGRATULATIONS!!

For Parents & Instructors:

For Certification, Coaching, Seminars, and Training, click on the Anti-bullying links above.

The Bullies Be Gone! Project Objective:

Self-Empowerment Training for Children and Teens That Prevents and Protects Against Bullying

You have now become Self-Empowered!

Your Instructor will Hand out Certificates of Completion and Trophies won for poetic performances. (Parent/Teacher Discretion)

END OF LESSON 8 AND THE EIGHT-WEEK COMPREHENSIVE TRAINING

www.ingramcontent.com/pod-product-compliance
Lightning Source LLC
Chambersburg PA
CBHW081354080526
44588CB00016B/2498